First Kiss

Eternal Echoes: The Initial And Final Touch Of Their Lips. An Account Of Intense Emotion, Predetermined Fate, And An Enduring Love That Transcends The Constraints Of Time

(A Standalone Romantic Comedy Spinoff Of The Shots On Goal Series)

Elias Kirk

For whatever reason, the cowboy implied that she didn't look like a lawyer; yet, his sister did apologize when he entered the kitchen.

"I apologize for Gavin. I don't know what else can be said about him other than that he's just country.

Lucy forced a laugh. That's alright. A man has previously believed that I was the legal secretary.

"Come on, Gavin! "This woman's time is being wasted," Kayla yelled into the other room.

Reentering the living room, the large, handsome man with an attitude to match took a beer. He took a seat across from his sister. He turned to face Lucy without saying anything. How come you would like to work for free on this? What benefits do you see?

His directness surprised Lucy, but she tried not to show it. "I enjoy being of assistance to others. I particularly enjoy lending a helping hand to those whom I believe the government is abusing.

"One impoverished country folk at a time, saving the world huh?"

Kayla gave him a rib-cracking elbow.

He continued, seemingly unfazed, saying, "You don't look that old." Are you a recent attorney?

Once more, his sister attempted to prod him, but he stepped away from her without looking away from Lucy's face. She was resolved not to let him know that he was giving her anxiety, even though it was unsettling.

"My age is twenty-nine," she said. "I've been practicing law for the past five years. I have been employed by a well established company for five years. I have more experience than many seasoned lawyers.

Gavin started drinking his beer slowly, and as he was doing so, his sister added, "Lucy, you mentioned that you've already reviewed the court filings. Could you perhaps let us know what kind of opportunity we have here?

Lucy gave Gavin a quick look. He continued to observe her. She returned her emerald eyes to his sister's countenance. Their faces were very similar, but when she looked at Kayla, it was easier for her to think clearly.

"Well, I reviewed every surveyor's file from the original time your family purchased this land." Sadly, Stevenson is correct in saying that the survey was not completed properly. It looked like this happened a lot around that period. I'm not sure why, but I'm assuming that money and politics had a role. However, Texas has additional laws in place that will assist us in combating that. Adverse Possession Law is one of such.

"Improper Possession? Is it comparable to squatters' rights? Gavin queried.

Sort of. According to the law, if someone enters a piece of property without authorization and trespasses there for a predetermined amount of years in a "open and notorious" manner, which is to say—

Gavin spat out, "We're not dumb; we're country." We become "notoriety and open."

Lucy cleared her throat, and Kayla gave her brother a fierce look. "As previously said, the mere act of physically occupying property that is not legally yours for a number of years in a row and in a conspicuous manner might confer upon the occupant the right to become the legal owner of that property. That time span is five years in Texas.

With excitement, Kayla remarked, "Well, we've been here a lot longer than five years." Gavin's eyebrows were furrowed. At last, he looked away from Lucy's face and fixed his gaze on his sister.

She said that she wants us to appear in court and claim that, Kay, we have been trespassing on this property for years. This land belongs to our family. The men who toiled and perspired for this land were my grandfather, his father, and our father. They didn't occupy it negatively. They used money, blood, and labor to pay for it.

"Mr. Walker, I don't mean to make light of the efforts your family made to acquire their land. My only goal is to support you in keeping it.

Gavin declared, "I'm not going to go into open court and say that I'm a trespasser on someone's land!" after getting up and emptying the beer bottle. This territory belongs to me. He gave Kayla a look. "Kay, this is our land."

His sister reassured him, "Right now, Gavin, but if we just go into that courthouse and say, 'This is our land!'" I worry that won't be sufficient. Everything will be lost for us. Lucy is attempting to assist us.

Glancing back to Lucy, Gavin continued, "I still don't see what you get out of this."

"Knowing that I was able to assist someone who deserved it gives me satisfaction."

And why do you believe we are deserving of it? Gavin queried.

Lucy sprang to her feet and grabbed her purse. She gave Kayla a gentle glance before turning her gaze back to her brother. "I firmly believe that your sister deserves my assistance. The verdict is still out on whether or not you do, I would have to say. I really appreciate you talking with me, Kayla. My number is with you. I'll be in Cross River tonight, and I'll make plans to remain as long as necessary if you decide you need my assistance. She turned to face Gavin, who appeared to be grinning slightly at the corners of his lips. "Mr. Walker, it was a pleasure to meet you."

Lucy brushed by him and headed for the door.

Kayla went after it. "Lucy, please assist me. In the morning, I'll give you a call.

Lucy gave a nod. "I would like to visit the area when it is not too near dusk in order to take some pictures of the disputed land."

Without a doubt, Kayla replied. "Tomorrow morning is going to be ideal. I appreciate you coming out so much, and I apologize for my brother's rudeness. Compared to people, he gets along much better with animals.

Lucy turned to smile as she walked away.

Gavin exclaimed, "Don't apologize for me like I'm a child," after Lucy had left.

Then stop acting like a little kid. Gavin, wow! You treated her as though she were the one coming to take our land away, but she is helping us with her time and money just because she is a wonderful person!

"Kayla, we don't know her. She might be here specifically for that reason. She wants to wander around on our property. She is speaking as though we are foolish.

Oh, please give up! She wasn't. All she was doing was attempting to make sense of things for us. As for me, I was grateful for it.

Actually, I didn't. I don't require her assistance.

"All right, clever guy, so tell me how we're going to take on the state of Texas while we're fighting to maintain this ranch and repel Tuck's attacks." When Gavin remained silent for a few seconds, Kayla went on, "I thought so. I need to go get something to eat.

He saw his sister walk over to the rear door and put on her rubber boots while he stood there. She was accurate. He was still unsure about how to preserve their land. However, he was certain that he wasn't prepared to put his trust in anyone else to do the job.

"I intend to complete my tasks prior to the sun setting." I need to check the fences since we have to move the animals out of the holding pens and back into the pasture tomorrow. I also believe that Chestnut is almost ready to foal. Today, I want to capture her, bring her inside, and place her in the stables. That is, if there are no further meetings that I am required to attend.

She got up and grabbed the door handle, saying, "Not today." But until this is done, you'll be at the next one and the one after that. Gavin, you're a landowner, not just a cowboy, and you better start acting like one, or else there won't be any land left for us to leave for our children. As she left, she shut the door firmly.

Gavin walked out the front door, tossing the beer bottle in the trash. By the door, Satan was waiting for him. He mounted the horse and gave a tongue-click. Kayla tossed hay into the holding kennels without looking up at them. She would get over it, even though she was furious. She would eventually realize that he was simply shielding them. He was confident that the attractive redhead legal woman would reveal her true nature, and Kayla would be grateful that her older brother was watching out for her.

Hearing a car approaching the drive, he began to walk out to the east field with the dogs and the goat. He came to a stop and bided his time till the pickup crossed the little slope that led to the main house. It was a brand-new Ford F-350 lifted six inches. Although he was unable to identify the truck, Brance Duncan, the driver, had been his accomplice since the second grade. After parking the eye-catching red pickup in front of the house, Brance got out. He went over to where Gavin and Satan were sitting and watching him, bending down to pet the dogs and goat that had come up to say hello.

"Hi, Mongoose!" You don't appear pleased to see me.

Smiling at his old friend, Gavin slid from the horse. "It's been so long since I last saw you that I forgot how you looked."

After that

"Classmate Malfoy, I know you're a good person!"

This one statement is like thunder roaring through the night sky.

He genuinely wanted to remark, "You're even more stupid than I am," NaamahNaamah.

But having grown up in an aristocratic household, he was naturally reluctant to mention anything that would cast doubt on his identity. He simply gave her a scowl while observing her naive, large eyes flutter.

"Classmate Malfoy, do I look particularly beautiful today?" She finally removed the box from his grasp, her expression solemn and devoid of any indication of humor.

Are there weeds all over your brain? With a frown, Draco's elegant brows knitted as he unwillingly dismissed her.

Miyeon hesitated a little bit: "So why are you giving me such a brilliant eyeball stare? Do you not see that we are surrounded? I'm not sure, but I believe you have a false impression of me."

There are a lot of people surrounding them right now, and Miyeon doesn't want to speak quietly.

As a result, Draco was unhappy to discover that he was truly encircled and that Potter's three ancestors could even be heard laughing nearby.

With his steely eyes, Draco arched his brow even further and darted around, causing the priest's focus to falter momentarily. Everything functions quite fine.

The sound interrupted itself, but it still didn't pause and reached the middle ear.

"That one is NaamahNaamah, quickly! I informed her that one of the reasons a scholar was eager to come here as the incorrect manager was "Still, isn't she fond of your fortunate old horse? Once more, she appears to be older!"

"Ben, judging by how much they talk, it's definitely a fruitless attempt to switch goals. Once more, they claim that if people don't take excellent care of them, they'll have to bring a draft to the door to feed the elderly cow.

"Slytherin really turned out to be a pervert, no wonder a bunch of them are yin and yang monsters"

Despite Hufflepuff and Gryfindor's near-provocation, Draco's demeanor did not change as he watched Naamah.

turned, as though she was not the subject of the debate.

He was quite surprised because, to him, Naamah seemed to Extremely irritable, when did she start to exhibit such unpleasant ripples?

Draco seemed a little astonished as the girl's delicate face was highlighted by the blue-gray pupils.

This woman will always be so stunning.

Previously, he didn't pay close attention to her; when she returned to look for her, he simply detested having to keep his distance. However, this is still the first opportunity he's had to get to know her and assess her.

Her lovely eyebrows were hidden beneath the pair of Hong BaoThach, and her eyes seemed to be filled with light. She had long hair in the back, covered in a green silk ribbon that was gradually turning white as snow. She was unable to talk, but she was still dancing and moving. hearts.

Draco felt his face heat up as he looked at it.

It is hard to deny that Naamah is more beautiful than he has ever seen; a noble girl her age had to be somewhat more attractive, and the fact that she apologizes to her is undeniably beautiful. At first sight, Naamah seemed gloomy, but in reality, she was once beautiful. She just regretted that years of unfulfilled love had left her bitter. In contrast to the past, Miyeon's current physical state is normal at nineteen years old, with her natural beauty and resentment aura fully veiled.

She followed Miyeon gently and naturally, bowing, but absolutely disoriented, as this euphoria did not last long. The same unwavering tone as always was used: "No matter how you say it, classmate Malfoy, thank you for helping me bring my luggage here." This words of gratitude choked the enraged Draco because it was the so-called right not to hit the smiling face.

regarding

His hand began to itch as soon as he glanced at his own staff. Hao desired to strike a person. He opened his mouth to say anything to calm this kind of feeling, when Boatrica's regal yet disloyal voice came from across the hall: "Hello! Welcome to Hogwarts, new year's pupils."

The Hogwarts welcome ceremony has already started disrespectfully.

Miyeon felt that it was incredibly horrible for her to disregard the principal on her first day of work, so she didn't need to be late for advise because she recalled Boatrica. She then brought her imaginary suitcase to the front hall. A single foot entered.

"I walked in with one foot, I wasn't late, but classmate Malfoy congratulated you on your late arrival, becoming the new manager of Hogwarts, I thought to you," he said, turning to face Draco with a brilliant smile on his face as he considered it. "The detention room welcomes you."

" %&#$¥£ It is difficult to define mental activities with words used by humans; this is Draco at this moment. To translate "NaamahNaamah how are you not dead, just die" would be as simple as that.

Historical Letters

The date on the postmark is May 14, 1944. Oh my, Grammy would have only been eighteen then, almost nineteen. Even though I'm a little awkward about prying into Grammy's private life, I manage to remove the delicate paper from the envelope.

You probably never imagined that I would write, yet here I am, my lovely English Rose, and all because I just can't seem to get you out of my brain.

Who would have guessed? I can't stop thinking about you after spending a night dancing with you at the USO club. On Saturday, I had no intention of going at all. I missed my family back home in the United States and didn't want to be here in England.

Life is weird that way. I would never have met my English Rose with the golden hair and brilliant blue eyes if my mates hadn't demanded that I accompany them instead of languishing in self-pity.

As soon as I stepped in, you caught my attention. You were laughing and enjoying yourself while seated with several pals. You invited us to sit at your table, and it seemed petty to hold onto my sorrows amid such cheerful companionship.

Even though I don't usually dance, I had to beg to have some alone time with you. I'm not skilled enough to be considered a dancer, but while you were in my arms, I felt like I was floating. You never stopped laughing or smiling, and the room was illuminated by the twinkle in your baby blues, even when I stepped on your toes. I believe I may have developed a slight romantic interest in you at that time.

My blues were banished by those few dances. Now that I'm back at camp, all I can think about is you.

I will understand if you don't write back, but I really hope you do.

Marlon

Whoa, Grammy had a wartime admirer. My gaze dropped to the picture. Is that dude Marlon? I'm eager to learn more. I reach quickly for the next letter, dated June 22, 1944.

I, a poor guy from Brooklyn and the son of a shopkeeper, hoped and never thought you would write me back, my lovely English Rose. I worry that responding to all of your queries will take up this entire letter.

Your initial inquiry concerned my origins, to which I have previously responded, but allow me to elaborate: Brooklyn is a city in New York. Indeed, I sincerely wish to return there in the future—as much as one can in this insane world.

Despite being in the air force, I'm not a pilot—that's something very different. I therefore cannot declare myself to be among the heroes who supported the D-Day landings by air.

As a mechanic, I dedicate all of my time to maintaining those aircraft in the air. Last year, I had wanted to enroll in college to study electrical engineering, but as it is, I'm employed in a different capacity. No, I don't want to think that way in case I jinx things. Perhaps when the war is finished.

Hearing about your family was fascinating. Isn't it ironic that your father, like mine, is a retailer? I was sorry to learn that your mother had passed away when you were little. Your older sister must have found it difficult to take on her role.

Although she is younger than I am and is still in high school, I also have a sister. Although my mother wants her to become a nurse, she is more interested in joining the military after graduation. The next time I write, I'll inform her about your job as a chauffeur for the upper echelons of the brass; I have no doubt that she would prefer to work in a similar capacity.

I'll be able to visit London again at the end of July. If I don't hear from you before then, I'll keep an eye out for you at the USO.

With the utmost respect,
Marlon

My mind is racing. Grammy was corresponding with Marlon, attempting to get to know him, rather than just being an admirer. The mail I take up after that is smaller and without a postmark.

My lovely English rose,

Having to go through the censors and all, I wasn't sure if my response to your letter would reach you in time when I received it. I'm asking a friend from home for a favor. He says he will drop it off at your headquarters. He drives for the big shots in the air force.

I will recognize you if we cross paths at the station since I will always carry a deep emotional connection to you. I have scheduled my leave for the final weekend of July. On Friday, we arrive by train at approximately 4 p.m. I could take you out to supper, maybe.

I'll head to the USO where we met on Saturday night just in case we don't see each other at the station.

I'm keeping track of the minutes until our next meeting.

Marlon

Did they get together? The letter that follows is dated August 5, 1944. I'm trying everything not to rip it out of its envelope.

My sweet English Rose,

When I saw you waiting on the platform, still wearing your uniform, and stretching your neck to find me, my heart pounded in my chest. I'm glad I'm tall because I soon found you practically lost in the throng, but my gaze never strayed from you, and before long, we were together.

I had to tell myself that we have only recently met, yet even though I feel like I know you so well, I still wanted to embrace and kiss you.

I was content with the way your face brightened up when I showed up, and my pulse raced as you put your arm through mine, leaned in, and said, "Hello, airman," in your gorgeous accent. How about taking a female out to dinner?

Though, to be honest, I would have been content to stare at you across the table. I wasn't sure whether we would talk much during our lunch. We didn't stop talking to give the waiter our order and for me to pay the bill, so I didn't need to worry.

How I wished the night would never end. Reluctant to let you go, I accompanied you to the subterranean since you had to go home before curfew. I got you to commit to meet the next day so you could show me around London before you departed.

My Rose, those views were nothing compared to you. Even if there had not been a battle going on, you would have exceeded all I saw that day, despite what you may have told me.

Being apart from my family is now more than manageable thanks to the two days I spent with you, Rose, and I feel really fortunate to have met you. I'm hoping you share my sentiments.

Until our next meeting, Marlon

Oh my god, throughout the war, Grammy was in love with someone else. It was like reading a love story when you read the notes Marlon wrote her. Why hadn't Grammy said anything? Was it that Grandpa never found out?

"That's not related to you at all." With a chilly smile, Andrew said, "She can live anywhere she wants." Keep out of my house and keep my eyes clean."

You were too forgiving yesterday if you didn't chase her away right away.

Ahead on the road, there was a person who went by during their conversation.

A young woman in a white dress emerged from Andrew's home.

It's Kate.

She donned white sneakers, lifted the corner of her skirt, and walked gingerly because the road was not easy.

She lifted her head just in time to view her face as the morning breeze blew past, her cheeks glowing with the sun's warmth and her eyes clear.

Adam caught his breath for a second, taken aback. He was a good distance away, but he could still feel the vibration of the beauty.

That fairy is this one!

"You... Andrew, how come you have the audacity to dismiss this teacher even though she is so lovely?"

If he's at home, he'll be content to stare at him; otherwise, he has to set up circumstances for other people.

Whether or not this girl is attractive... Andrew paid no mind to it.

Adam, this coward, is done for.

"It doesn't appear to be that big." Adam started talking again.

He said this while keeping his gaze fixed on Kate, watching her go forward and never taking his eyes off hers.

Kate had no idea what she had walked on at the time. Her entire body became unsteady as she abruptly twisted her leg, causing her to fall to the ground.

Due to its narrowness and steepness, this path is difficult to traverse and can quickly topple those who are unfamiliar with it.

However, the residents of the town have long since adapted to it.

She made a knee scrape.
Kate's eyes started to go crimson around the edges at this point.
This time it aches, really, truly hurts.
Sharp rocks are everywhere on the road.
You can probably tell that your knee is fractured without ever looking.
Sniffling, she told herself she would not display her messy appearance when she went to class.
Andrew turned around, appeared bored, and was ready to walk away.
His feet ceased as soon as he turned around, and the corners of his eyes brightened. Not knowing what to believe, he turned around.
Kate continued walking forward.
Her movements are light and airy, the hem of the tight white dress slightly elevated, and the outfit merely accentuates her slender waist. She pushed through the agony and started to run slowly on a rather level route.
The rear swiftly slipped from view.

It was obvious that the guy had left because the previous figure had suddenly reappeared in front of him.

With his lips pursed and the bottoms of his eyes chilly, Andrew uttered a low-pitched curse, "Fuck!"

The eighth-grade third-grader now has a lovely new homeroom instructor.

Beautiful appearance and kind disposition.

However, despite his beauty, the class president is unable to get the position.

Third graders in the eighth grade are notoriously rebellious, especially the ones with issues who subtly stir up trouble.

There is one hour of downtime following lunch. This is a unique moment of calm during the school day.

It's understandable to feel exhausted and desire to sleep during the summer. You will fall asleep even more after a full dinner.

Stepping onto the bench next him, Leon pounded on the tables of the two individuals seated next to him before yelling, "Go, go outside and play."

Reluctant to get up, Ly Tu Chan and Ly Thuy yawned drowsily and cautiously responded, "It's lunch break right now, it's not good..."

This year, Leon is the eldest student in the class at fifteen, making him the most conceited and acerbic.

Without skipping a beat, he continued speaking and said bluntly, "Is there something wrong, are you still afraid?"

He didn't feel scared.

I was courageous before, but now I'm even more bold and unafraid.

The two of us could only follow him out; there was no other option.

The door's security guy was just partially awake. The children softly opened the door and fled when he was not looking.

Since the weather is so lovely, playing in the water is obviously quite appropriate. There is a river close to the school; the water is shallow and moves slowly. Everyone has enjoyed playing by the river since they were young. Occasionally, they will swim a few laps in peace.

It goes without saying that in this type of summer weather, the river water is chilly.

We three have no idea how long we played for.

They carried their shoes to a tree's shade to rest when they grew tired of playing.

Ly Thuy sprung to her feet in a horrified voice before her butt had had time to warm up: "There's a snake!"

When Leon's face went white from fear, he was lying nonchalantly. When he looked back, he spotted a snake slithering on the grass right next to him.

Leon felt instantly paralyzed by a cold sensation across his body.

Even more perplexed were the other two.

Nobody reacted fast enough, and everyone had a small liver.

At that very time, out of nowhere and with swift motions, a hand reached out to grasp the snake.

Andrew was the one who chance to walk by.

Standing idly by the tree, he glanced at the snake he was holding and then laughed, asking, "Are you losing face?"

"This one isn't poisonous, it's so scary that it makes me pee my pants."

Phung Du took a deep breath. It took him many seconds to respond. He was having trouble looking up.

Upon glancing at the snake grasped by Andrew, his fear returned.

"Leaving school early?" Andrew posed a casual query as he turned to face the nearby high school.

The children were silent and in disbelief. Throwing the snake into the river, Andrew took a step forward.

"Don't skip school when you're young, come back quickly!"

After saying something brief, Andrew raised his foot and moved ahead.

Leon didn't respond until then. He got up and swiftly crept on the ground. After pursuing Andrew, he exclaimed, "Brother, you are so amazing!" in amazement.

People find it difficult to taunt Andrew simply by glancing at him because of his innate gangster mentality.

This person will be the most worshipped by those Leon's age.

"What are you doing, brother?" Leon trailed after him, inquiring.

"It is not ideal to do nothing."

"Brother, may I trail you?" Leon thought, "I will definitely be able to run wild at school in the future if I can recognize someone like this as my brother!"

So attractive, so vicious!

See if the older students in your grade still have the courage to approach you.

"Impossible." Andrew accelerated his pace, ignoring the children.

After a while of Leon stalking him, Andrew abruptly stopped and asked, "Do you want me to report it to your teacher?" in a stern voice.

What an annoying brat.

But Leon told himself that he wouldn't be worried if he just told the teacher.

Eventually, Leon was unable to keep up.

"What's your name, honey?" With a loud cry, Leon posed a query.

Andrew remained silent.

"That's Andrew." Ly Thuy caught up at this point as well, turned to face Andrew, and remained silent for a moment.

Although the Demon King of Chaos enjoys a stellar reputation in New York, his negative image is so widespread that hardly anyone is unaware of him.

I heard that yesterday was your homecoming to New York.

All of a sudden, Leon woke up and realized.

Whoa, that illustrious Andrew really is strong!

"I will definitely follow him in the future," Leon replied in silence.

..

When Trinh Phong returned in the afternoon, Mrs. Eva took him aside right away.

"Have you not said anything to Kate?"

"This morning she told her she wanted to move," inquired Mrs. Eva.

Andrew would not have wanted to move out when he first moved in, Mrs. Eva had already surmised that he must have said something.

Andrew remained silent.

He was leaning against the table, appearing lethargic, with his eyes downcast and somewhat icy at the corners.

Your appearance is regarded as an implicit admission.

Helplessly, Mrs. Eva shook her head.

Although my nephew has a bad reputation and a bad personality in New York, only Mrs. Eva is aware of his nice nature.

"She has a home here, so it's good for her to live here."

Following a brief pause, Mrs. Eva said, "Kate is obedient and understanding, and being able to be with her in her arms makes her very happy."

We barely make it into the room when we get to his floor before we start ripping each other's clothes off. He releases his hold on my neck and puts on a condom. I can feel the excitement building inside me because I know he plans to finish this time.

He looks at me as if he's not sure where to begin. I sit down on the bed and let my panties fall to the floor.

"You requested cake." I tell him, pushing myself back with my legs spread wide.

Falling to his knees, Bryce assumes the role of a competitor in a food-eating competition. My ears are ringing with anticipation.

"How in the world is that?" Bryce enquired.

My stomach turns over.

When a man is face down in his pussy, that is the last thing I want to hear, what the heck is that? He's staring at me with wide, worried eyes when I sit up.

Oh no.

I rest my head back on the bed.

Excitement isn't ringing in my ears. It's the hall's high-pitched fire alarm going off.

I reassure him, "It's probably nothing," as I attempt to get his head back between my knees.

We have experienced false alarms from our fire alarm before. Usually, there's someone smoking in a room, or perhaps there's something a touch too smokey that someone produced in the kitchen.

When my phone starts ringing, I start to worry that there might be a more serious issue.

I get out of Bryce's bed and pick up my phone.

"Hey, I'll be down shortly. Give me a short while.

Bryce sits on the floor at the foot of the bed and puts his hands over his head. His expression turns disappointed, but there's nothing I can do.

"Do I have to leave?" Bryce queries.

At the reception, it seemed like sparklers were lighted. The restaurant started to smell a little smokey.

"That seems like a manageable task." I put on my panties again and he crawls over to me.

There was something about watching Bryce on his hands and knees pleading with me to keep my fires lit. This man crawls to me and begs me to stay, even though he could have anything and anyone. This stuff completely blows my mind.

I clarify, "It's a new employee working tonight." "He seems a little worried. I'll return after everything has been resolved.

Even though I was determined to follow through on my commitment, I never return to Bryce's room. I'm worn out by the time I assist the front desk employee in tending to all of the anxious guests. I go directly to my room and don't even think about Bryce till I pass out.

***

The restaurant has already been returned to its former design and layout by the next morning. This time of day is slow. When I see Gabe, Tiffany, James, and Shade seated at a table, I'm taken aback. They give me a wave. Raising up, Gabe grabs a chair from across the table and places it between Tiffany and Shade on the end of the four top.

"Good morning, everyone."

Muffled good mornings resound. I see that the previous evening, they were all a little rough. They couldn't have stayed long because they haven't placed an order yet.

"What did I miss?" I inquire.

"Not really," Shade responds. "They were merely discussing their impending honeymoon."

"When do you guys depart once more?" Gabe queries the recentlyweds.

"Next week," Tiffany says with a smile. "I get to have him all to myself at last, getting to pull him away from work."

I sincerely agree and nod. When it comes to work, James is worse than I am.

Before they go, she wants to go bowling as a pair. Shade gives an eye roll.

My ears prickle. I adore playing bowling. We were on the same league as my spouse before he died away. Even though it's been a while, I think I still understand.

James says, "You should come too, Denise."

Of all people, James knows how much I love to bowl. He saw to ensure that I left work early enough to attend our league nights.

I turn down the invitation with a shake of my head. "I wish not to be the sidekick."

They ought to comprehend. Nobody wants to be the lone single person going out with other couples.

"Perhaps Bryce will wish to attend as well." Shading glances at me, Shade informs Tiffany.

Gabe gives her a prod. She stops laughing and droops her head. I sling daggers at her, my eyes narrowing.

We have a strictly sexual agreement, but Bryce seems cool. But it appears that fate has other ideas. Something manages to cut things short every time we get rolling.

Yes, indeed. That's a really good concept," Tiffany says with a smile, completely oblivious to the surrounding nonverbal exchange. "I believe he has a few more days left in town. Allow me to question him.

Gabe responds, "I don't think we should put him on the spot like that."

I thank him in silence for attempting to save me from more anguish and embarrassment as my eyes soften in his way.

"That's crazy," scoffs Tiffany. "He will adore it."

Gabe's eyebrows furrow regretfully. He made an attempt.

With complete assurance, Tiffany responds, "He'll come."

Shade sees farther than I do. Allow him to respond to himself. She gestures for someone to come along with her waves.

I can tell who she's inviting over without turning around. James gets to his feet and moves a chair to the other end of the table. Bryce strolls by me, leaving a trail of his heady perfume behind.

"Good morning, everyone." My gaze is drawn to his lips by his rich, deep voice.

My mind replays another cut-off moment from the previous evening. As he tells me what he's about to do to me, I see him getting in close and kissing my earlobes. where the tip of his tongue will go.

Appearing incredibly attractive, he takes a seat between James and Gabe across the table. More combined than all of us put together. He reclines on his chair with a confident, carefree swagger. He nods his head slightly upward toward me.

"Bryce, would you like to join us tomorrow night for some bowling?" Shade dives straight in.

"I'm not feeling well." He doesn't think twice about it.

Tiffany becomes excited. You see, I told you. In bowling, Bryce is not competitive.

Shade's cunning gaze is constantly darting from Bryce to me.

James adds his voice. Denise, you must now arrive. Bryce must be included; else, he would be the fifth wheel.

With close eye contact, Bryce says, "You can't leave me hanging," which makes me think of something sexual again.

I force myself to look away from his captivating stare in an attempt to divert my attention from the need to entice him away from this late meal and experience a complete encounter with him.

My legs splayed apart. Our bodies were squeezed together. Sweat combining as we ride the passion wave to the top.

"Are you coming?" With a question that brings me back to the present, Bryce asks.

"I said, my voice sounding hollow in my own ears, "It's not weird." I prayed the untruth escaped their ears. "We had a history of our own, but that was a long time ago."

"Happy to hear it," Emmett remarked. At the very least, a few days, I believe he will be here. The guy was, after all, grocery shopping.

I got Gracie's attention. She was keeping a worried eye on me. She was aware that I never fully moved on from Brayden, even if she was unaware of how deeply his departure had affected me. I tried to reassure her that everything was well by giving her a tiny grin.

"I'm hungry," I murmured. "You guys are aware of your desires?"

I flagged down our server after they both nodded at me, and we all placed our orders. Then we sat around talking about less interesting stuff while I enjoyed the warmth of the fire at my back. We discussed the endless snow, the weather, my artwork, Gracie's yoga, and Emmett's ongoing struggle to get extra ketchup for his eatery. Ketchup was one of the items that was hard to import into Valdez for some odd reason.

I laughed and added, "I don't think you'll lose customers because you're temporarily out of ketchup."

Emmett ran a hand over his red hair. "You have no idea how traditional the elderly residents of this town are, girl. They don't want fries if they don't come with ketchup. They have the ability to destroy my company.

"More than ketchup?" I questioned in disbelief.

Above anything they find intolerable. This week, ketchup is in.

I explained, "This is why I paint."

After a good chuckle from all of us, our appetizers quickly arrived. While we ate, we talked, and Emmett muttered something about how the Tavern still had an excess of ketchup. All was well in Gracie's world until she suddenly gasped loudly and dropped her French fry.

"Oh sh*t," she said.

"What?" I looked up at her and inquired.

She was gazing toward the front doors, past Emmett. I followed her line of sight until I saw a tall, dark-haired man shrugging out of a black, knee-length winter jacket that was far too formal for a town like Valdez. After taking off his gloves, he stuffed them into the jacket's pockets and hung the item on a hook to his right.

Then, with his hands rubbing together, he turned to face the bar, and my heart leaped into my throat.

It seems as though BraydenHennie was sex wrapped in sex and then dipped in more sex.

I forcefully gulped.

Emmett raised his arm in the air, glancing over his shoulder to point out our table to Brayden. He turned to walk in our direction.

Oh my god. Holy fucking crap. Be ordinary. Be ordinary. My heart began to race, and I grabbed a napkin from the table to wipe my mouth, fearing that something oily or sauced had gotten on it.

Gracie gave me a puzzled glance and muttered, "How did he get hotter?"

With a shrug and my heart racing a mile per minute, I turned right as Brayden pulled up next to our table.

I took in every moment of seeing him as he greeted Emmett with a pat on the back. I had to wait a minute for him to look at me directly before I realized how dramatically he had changed.

He seemed taller than I had recalled. His dark blue jeans fit him just right, too perfect to be the kind of jeans you'd find on a Valdez store shelf. The black watch on his left wrist and the black shirt tucked under his belt also gave off an opulent appearance, as did his boots.

On his jaw and neck, where he had failed to grow facial hair the previous time I saw him, was heavy stubble. He had grown into a man. A mature, strong, broad-shouldered man whose presence was making me feel a kind of primordial familiarity beneath my stomach.

"I'm going to sell this house.

There must be something wrong with my hearing. This is what happens when I spend a long, wet day at school eating nothing but a school cafeteria cheeseburger all day.

"What did you say?" I want to know exactly what Joe means.

"Skye."

Really, though, I didn't understand that. How did you say that? I inquire idly.

Joe says again, "I said I'm selling this place."

I therefore do not have hearing loss. That is exactly what he said, and he appears to be taking it seriously. Joe is aware enough not to tamper with such matters.

"What on earth does that mean?"

We're losing a lot of money here, Skye. You are aware of it. We require assistance—

"Joe, what the fuck?" I respond. "What in the world are you discussing?

How would selling this property help us with our financial issues?

"Relax, this isn't a total sell-off. Simply put, the new person has a big stake. I struck a deal with him, and you will continue to be in charge of...

"JOE! You sold this home and kept me in the dark about it?

"It's okay, I didn't tell you because I anticipated your reaction. In order to best serve this place, I had to make an executive choice. Skye, I'll be retiring soon. A chance presented itself, and I had to seize it.

"Oh, so after you sell this home, you're just going to take off? To go whaling, is that what?

This isn't 'running off.' I simply...All I need is a little vacation. Skye, I'm very sorry that this came as a complete surprise. However, I was unable to turn down the opportunity to preserve this site.

The man in front of me doesn't sound like the father who reared me and died in love with this country, and this is so incredibly stupid. Is he selling? "What have you done with my Joe Holiday, and who are you?"

"Hey Skye.

What is the duration of your planning for this? And who the hell is the buyer? Why won't you communicate with me? Joe, what the fuck is this? Speak with me!

"Devon Gray," mumbles. "Devon Gray is buying this place from me."

There must be a clever joke behind this. There is no fucking sense to anything that has been said in the last two minutes. Devon Gray would never be the buyer of Joe's family business. He would never do anything without informing me first.

"Why would you act in that way? You've only met Devon Gray once, so you don't really know him. And he and his friends stayed here more than a month ago. Technically, twice, if the day of the truck accident is included.

Please listen to me, Skye. Indeed, he spent that evening here with his pals. He asked to meet with me in private the following morning. You must have remembered that.

Yes, I reply. But you told me that he spoke with you privately to voice his displeasure with the plumbing.

Yes, but that wasn't the only thing. I declined his offer to purchase this property. He made it. However, Joe says, grabbing my hand, "Skye." "I researched him and thought about it for a while. He's a bright young man with the means and the ideas to make this town better. We require his assistance. If we don't, this place won't make it through this season."

"I disagree with you, Joe," I reclaim my hand. "If this has to do with money, I'll handle it."

"You can't be allowed to do that. You have bills to pay as a college student.

Joe, we're not in poverty. Of all people, you are aware that business slows down during the spring. If we simply wait it out, things will get better.

Chapter 7: Linking the dots

The relationship between Emma and Luke continued to grow as the days turned into weeks, like a tide gradually rising to the shore. What had started off as an unexpected encounter had developed into a fascinating bond that they both cherished.

Their correspondence became a regular part of Emma's calendar. They would get together at the corresponding seaside bistro and have easily communicative conversations. Emma discovered that in addition to being a close friend, Luke was a guy of mystery. Throughout his daily existence, he was passionate about workmanship, adored the beach, and yearning for something more.

Their conversations were more often about the imaginations they had explored deeply within themselves than they were about their personal mysteries and desires. Luke encouraged Emma to rekindle her passions, which had been overshadowed by the comforting bond she shared with Imprint. Thus, Emma gave Luke the motivation to confront his history and confront the demonic spirits he had been avoiding.

As time went on, Emma's interest in Luke grew, and she sensed that he had the same feelings. Their relationship was significant, an underlying pull that brought them closer. But they walked carefully around the clear science between them, understanding that following their feelings would have consequences.

Tension began to show in Emma's relationship with Imprint. Luke gradually took over her thoughts, and she found herself comparing the energy she experienced with him to the stability and commonality she gave Stamp.

They happened upon a secret inlet—a secluded area where it seemed as though the world disappeared—while strolling beside the sea one evening. They experienced a moment of vulnerability there, in the embrace of the ocean breeze and the thundering waves, with a covert kiss that left them speechless and wanting more.

Their kiss that sticks in your memory the most was electrifying, a sign of the fire that had ignited between them. It was a turning point, a border that neither could dispute. Right now, Emma's heart was split between the vitality she had found with Luke and the adoration she had felt for a while.

That night, as they parted ways, their hearts heavy with the weight of unspoken desires, they couldn't deny that something unusual had begun to unfold. Their growing intimacy had the potential to put their allegiances to the test, shake their principles, and take them in a direction neither of them had anticipated.

Getting Closer at Seabreeze Cove in Chapter 8

As time went on, Emma and Luke's bond deepened and became a kinship that the two felt was essential to their survival. Seabreeze Inlet served as the backdrop for their growing relationship with its enduring beauty and hidden wonders.

Together, they set off on adventures too great to measure, exploring the town's enchanted tiny secret places. Their evenings were spent exploring hidden stores, strolling down cobblestone streets, and sampling the town's delicious fish at local bistros. Every journey offered an opportunity to observe one another.

They made the decision to ascend the winding stairs of the beacon that had long since abandoned Seabreeze Inlet on a brilliant day. They were made up for their losses at the summit with a breathtaking view over the town and the vast expanse of the sea. There, surrounded by the pulsating melody of the beacon's pillar, they exchanged their dreams and anxieties, creating a bond that seemed as enduring as the sea itself.

Their safe sanctuary, where they could retreat from the outside world and behave naturally, was the oceanfront. They spent hours collecting shells, strolling along the shoreline together, and taking in the dusk's colorful sunsets that turned the sky a variety of pinks and oranges. Their hearts grew closer with every shared second, and their laughter perfumed the air.

As the midyear days wore on, Emma introduced Luke to the town's annual festivities and traditions. They marched beneath the stars at the live event by the coast, had picnics in the town square all through the late spring fair, and celebrated the Fourth of July by watching firecrackers light up the night sky. When they were together, Seabreeze Bay's magic seemed to intensify, making even the most effortless minutes seem extraordinary.

Their family were also touched by their growing affinity. Emma introduced Luke to her mother Beauty, and the two of them would often sit on the terrace at night, sipping tea, laughing, and exchanging stories. Luke replied by extending an invitation for Emma to meet his sister Rachel, who became an instant friend and deepened the group of people who had become so important to Emma.

Regardless, within the comparatively large number of mutual interactions and glances, there was an underlying force, a shared understanding of the indisputable science, present between them. They navigated the energy simmering beneath the surface, aware that acknowledging it would forever change the course of their lives.

Seabreeze Bay was no longer just a place; it was the canvas on which their relationship was drawn and the place where their emotions had been intertwined in a way that neither could ignore. The days of late spring were becoming hazy, and the winds of harvest time whispered secrets of advancement. Emma and Luke's relationship was about to undergo its most significant trial, and the path they were on would eventually bring them to a decisive moment.

The Bravery to Admit Oneself

In "The Journey of the First Kiss," Chapter 5, "The Courage to Step Forward," Jane and David are about to experience a turning point in their relationship. The boldness of expressing one's emotions, the dread of the unknown, and the beauty of vulnerability in love are all highlighted in this chapter.

Jane opens the chapter with mixed feelings of anxiety and excitement in her heart. She's made the decision to tell David how she really feels. Although she is afraid, she instinctively understands that she cannot carry on suppressing her feelings. She secretly thinks that David still has affections for her and longs for his understanding.

David is seen attempting to make sense of his perplexity in parallel. Although he is optimistic about Jane and Matt's breakup, he worries about the possible effects on their friendship. David isn't sure how Jane feels about him yet. Though his heart aches for Jane, he fears being turned down once more.

After that, the story moves to their high school. The school library is where Jane and David first meet, and it is there that their friendship has grown over time. Jane summons the bravery to resolve to take advantage of the situation. She chooses to tell David how she truly feels, her heart racing in her chest.

Jane opens up to David in a very personal session. She talks about her sentiments of uncertainty, realization, and remorse for not realizing them sooner. Her admission is sincere. David can't express how shocked he is by Jane's disclosure. His heart is racing with a mix of feelings as he looks at Jane, including relief, astonishment, and unwavering love.

In this chapter, David's response to Jane's confession is crucial. There is a startled stillness for a minute, and then he tells her that he still loves her. Their honest and emotional disclosure marks a sea change in their relationship.

The chapter ends on a somewhat somber note, despite their relief at finally putting their sentiments into words. It is now up to Jane and David to manage their changed relationship. They are excited by their shared emotions but also nervous about the potential changes.

David and Jane's relationship is about to take a new turn. After exposing their emotions, they set out on a brand-new adventure that is rife with excitement, anticipation, and just a hint of fear.

The story goes into greater detail about Jane and David's feelings after their admission. Jane begins to envisage a bright future for herself and David as she feels relieved and happy. She comes to the realization that her affections for David had always been firmly ingrained in her heart; she had just never acknowledged them before.

David, on the other hand, experiences a wave of happiness and relief after having to endure the heartbreak of unfulfilled love. His love for Jane, which he had previously believed to be unrequited, is returned. This newfound happiness is anxiously tempered, though. He worries about the future and is afraid of how their relationship dynamics may evolve.

Jane and David negotiate their new relationship in the days that follow their confession. They exchange hesitant looks and smiles, and there's a fresh, exhilarating tension in their chats. A lighthearted element is added to the story by their friends, who see the shift in their relationship and begin making fun of them.

Jane and David are excited, but they also have to redefine boundaries in their relationship. They struggle to make the transition from friends to more than friends since they don't know how to proceed in this unfamiliar area. Their friendship still has its familiarity and comforts, but it is now tinted with the excitement and unpredictability of passionate love.

As the chapter comes to a close, Jane and David make the decision to slow down their relationship. They agree to stay friends and allow their romantic relationship to grow organically. In a poignant moment, they pledge to support one another through thick and thin. Their hearts overflowing with love and hope, they clasp hands beneath the ancient oak tree as the narrative comes to a close.

Having just taken my permission slip from the nurse's office, I spot him in the waiting area.

Andrews, Dean.

The boy who is at the top of my list of people I detest and probably will be for eternity.

He was covered in liquid when I last saw him. He appears to have just gotten out of the shower based on how wet his chocolate brown hair is. He has also taken off his black top. He's now dressed in big brown corduroy slacks and a crimson shirt with a few holes in it.

It's obvious that Serena wasn't the only person who used Lost & Found.

If I wasn't so enraged, I would joke.

"You" I eventually get Dean's attention when I snarl. "All of it is your fault. On Tiktok, I'm becoming viral because of you.

The fact that I'm not sure if the video has truly gone viral is irrelevant, though. I harbor resentment for him.

"Me?" With a frown, he gestures to himself. "That entire thing was caused by you."

"You gave me a kiss!"

It happened by mistake. And I've already expressed my regret. Are his cheeks a touch pink, or am I seeing things differently?

"That is insufficient!"

Alright, difficult. I won't apologize once more.

We give each other a fierce look as though we're at a standoff.

I have no idea why he is so angry. I just responded to what he had done to me. Was I just meant to smile and get by? Forget about that. He won't get away with it from me.

"Jerk, you owe me."

He stays put, crossing his arms over his chest. "No, I don't believe so."

Just as I'm about to object, I hear the nurse's office door fly open behind me.

"Mr. Andrews, you may enter at this time."

My gaze narrows. Is he also attempting to obtain a permission slip? I had a very bright notion right then. Before Dean can say anything, I turn around. It's alright, Miss. He's feeling better already.

"What are you discussing?"

The blonde nurse in her twenties scowls at Dean's response.

However, I quickly draw her gaze back to myself. I give her a charming smile, using all the charm I possess. In any case, it was only a slight headache. He'll get by.

She gives a shrug. "All right, if you say so."

However, that's not the case.

Dean's speech is interrupted as the nurse retreats back inside her office and shuts the door.

With a victorious smile, I turn to face him once more. "You made a statement?"

He has a crimson face. He appears enraged. "How in the world was that? Your senseless reprisal?

Naturally, no. I had only barely begun.

His expression changes abruptly, going from anger to something else. Something hazardous. I had to take several steps back to avoid being pushed forward as he gets closer. "Oh, Hart, it's on." Then, leaving me staring after him, he exits the waiting area.

Has he declared war already?

I felt terrible as I said to her, "I know, I'm sorry."

Kindly cease doing that without apologizing! She went on, "Come on, you're better than that," but I ignored her. It didn't make it any easier when she continued, even though I knew she would have to say her fill and then be over it.

She started talking endlessly, so I eventually cut her off. Dear Marlow, I'm sorry. Nothing else is available to me. I was so tired that I said, "Either accept it or hang up, but I'm not going to listen anymore."

A minute passed in quiet. "You're accurate. I should have gotten the message to shut talking a lot sooner from you.

It was said and done, and even though we both laughed, I didn't feel like chatting anymore. I cut her off by telling her I had business to attend to. Mom had prepared peanut brittle and arranged a selection of cheese and crackers as our movie snack. Up until I started working, it was our regular pattern. However, when I began working on Saturday mornings, Marlow and Rachel worked most Saturday nights, so I was at home to carry on the custom.

I woke up smiling around four on Sunday morning. I was back at work with Nick. I took a shower, changed into my outfit, and tried to give my hair some curl. However, as fate would have it, I had to depart since I ran out of time.

I was ready to wait for Nick and Sam to get there when I got to the store, but the lights were on. It was not Sam's car that I spotted when I rounded the building to the back parking lot, but David's. I exhaled.

Nick smiled briefly as he approached the door, but his attention was diverted by his phone. He gave me a big smile as he opened the door. I slid past him, not wanting to disturb him, and made my way toward the back.

I heard Nick say, "Look, I don't know what more you want me to say," before I was out of hearing range. But I must let you leave because I have to go to work.

I checked in, got my apron, and went straight to the buffet containers. I didn't want David to have anything to justify his criticism of me. I wasn't very interested in interacting with him, not that he'd ever had any anyway.

I bent to retrieve the remaining containers after removing the first layer. I then heard a lengthy whistle and footsteps behind me. I hurried to stand, praying it was Nick and not David.

It was Nick. He leaned over and picked up the containers, asking, "Need help with that?"

"Yes, of course," I answered after he had already taken them up.

Nick placed the receptacles on the countertop and then faced me, maintaining the same demeanor from when he had opened the door. There was a problem. However, he asked, "How come I never see you with a phone?" before I had the chance to ask.

Though it was certainly not what I was expecting to hear, the question was intriguing enough. "I store it in my locker to avoid getting into trouble."

He chuckled. He said, taking his phone out of his back pocket, "Everyone carries their phone on them." His expression became solemn as he raised his head. "Rory, may I have your number?" he enquired.

"Oh, yeah," I exclaimed, really taken aback. Though that was the last thing I could have imagined, it made me very pleased. As he inserted my number into his phone, I rattled it off.

His fingers skimmed over his phone, then he said, "I'm going to text you, so you have my number too."

Wondering what he was going to text was going to be a long day. Would he genuinely say something, or would he merely send a letter at random? Yes, it will undoubtedly be a long shift!

By keeping ourselves occupied with work, we were able to extend our break by 10 minutes prior to the restaurant's opening. We grabbed our normal seats, and David joined us as we were about to eat.

"Is this just for lovers, or can I join you?" he asked himself, laughing uncontrollably.

"Oh, you can come along," Nick responded, moving to make room for him.

David took a seat and started to cram food into his lips. Which I found acceptable because I'd prefer he be too busy to speak with us. Unfortunately for me, though, he still managed to find time to speak.

He waved his fork between us and exclaimed, "So, are you two... hooking up?" or have you already connected?

Naturally, I was more surprised than Nick. He was close with David and had worked with him far more than I had. However, I had no affection for him at all. Nick only laughed when David inquired about hooking up. I became a gorgeous shade of scarlet.

David apologized for embarrassing you, he said with a convincing air.

Rather than brushing it off, I actually heard myself say, "Unless you're living vicariously through us, our sex life shouldn't be a concern of yours."

David's eyes grew wide, and a loud chuckle erupted from everyone. He turned to give Nick a quick shove. "She's quite the darling, isn't she?"

With a laugh, Nick remarked, "She's something, okay." He then grinned at me. The smile that conveys more.

Even though our break ended far sooner than I had planned, I was happy to start the day. Nick's message would arrive on my phone sooner rather than later as the shift progressed. The morning started out slowly before becoming busy. Nick spent most of the day closely monitoring his phone. He even made a few excuses to answer some of the numerous calls he got.

Every time he returned from a call, he seemed anxious. When our eyes met, he would always smile flirtatiously, but most of the time his face was hidden by a troubled expression. Though I hoped it had nothing to do with his family, it didn't seem to have anything to do with me, so I decided it was best to leave it alone.

I had two things I was looking forward to when our shift finally finished. Our lunch rendezvous and Nick's message. Not a date, exactly, but something.

I threw my apron in my locker, clocked out, and picked up my phone. Just one text message was sent. Naturally, Nick.

Nick: I've got yours and now you've got mine.

Cryptic much?Or just as simple as it's written. He's got my number and now I have his. Either way, I took the more meaningful implication because he certainly had my heart. I took a deep breath and let it out slowly and shoved the phone in my pocket.

As I turned around, Nick was right there in my space. So much that my forehead met his chin. "Oh my gosh, I'm sorry. Are you okay?" I asked.

He chuckled. "It didn't hurt. Are you ready?"

I didn't make an attempt to move away. Instead, I looked up into his gorgeous brown eyes. "Yeah," I replied.

He turned to the side of me and placed his hand on my lower back. "Do you mind if we go somewhere else? I'm not up to eating here after serving it all day."

Stunned by the fact that he wanted to go somewhere else, or perhaps, stunned because his hand was on my back...intimately. "Sure, whatever you want," I said a little breathier than I had wanted. It went unnoticed, or he ignored it, because he continued to walk me out to his car where he opened the door and settled me inside.

Throughout the night, Whitey imagined striking all five at once, with each one collapsing under his strikes. He want them all at once. The son repeatedly swung the sock in his thoughts. He was upset by the assault, so it was a restless night. He followed his customary route and went for school at the regular time. He crossed the brook when he came to a certain location along the railroad tracks. He looked from stone to stone, looking for a rock the size of a sweet potato. When he found one, he put the sweet potato in his pocket and traded it for the stone. Whitey followed his father's instructions, but he didn't think the potato could withstand the five. He took out the rock and threw it back into Loup Creek, replacing the sweet potato, after reaching the bank of the creek. "That may not have a satisfied dad if I didn't do it his way," he said out loud.

He witnessed the five walk inside his classroom through the corridor. He desired for them to be seated. All he had with him was the sock in his right hand. Though his enlarged left eye appeared closed, his right eye was still functional. Though he turned left to pass beside the five, the path to his seat was straight. He battered them and then followed the other students, easily making it to his location.

Everyone rushed toward the five as the room descended into chaos. The boy was bewildered, and Miss Bruce hesitated before acting. She sent a pupil go to pick up the principal. At last he entered, and the physician showed in a few minutes later. The physician determined they required hospitalization right away. Ambulances arrived shortly after and took them away. An ambulance arrived, and someone brought the boy to the principal's office.

When his mother arrived, she said nothing to him. It was not the right time to be upset, and she wasn't angry. So she just waited, watching.

Mr. Hensley demanded to know "why did you do this to those children" as he began questioning Whitey.

"I did nothing to those boys," he retorted.

One of the youngsters was the son of the school's principal, Mr. Hensley. "Miss Bruce, tell me what you saw."

"Whitey, why do you lie so much? Don't deny that I witnessed you hit those boys with that sock you had.

Sticking to his account, Whitey said, "I did not do it." One boy was invited to attend the meeting by Mr. Hensley. When Whitey attacked my son, Jerry, were you by his side?

"Yes, master."

Throughout the night, Whitey imagined striking all five at once, with each one collapsing under his strikes. He want them all at once. The son repeatedly swung the sock in his thoughts. He was upset by the assault, so it was a restless night. He followed his customary route and went for school at the regular time. He crossed the brook when he came to a certain location along the railroad tracks. He looked from stone to stone, looking for a rock the size of a sweet potato. When he found one, he put the sweet potato in his pocket and traded it for the stone. Whitey followed his father's instructions, but he didn't think the potato could withstand the five. He took out the rock and threw it back into Loup Creek, replacing the sweet potato, after reaching the bank of the creek. "That may not have a satisfied dad if I didn't do it his way," he said out loud.

He witnessed the five walk inside his classroom through the corridor. He desired for them to be seated. All he had with him was the sock in his right hand. Though his enlarged left eye appeared closed, his right eye was still functional.

Though he turned left to pass beside the five, the path to his seat was straight. He battered them and then followed the other students, easily making it to his location.

Everyone rushed toward the five as the room descended into chaos. The boy was bewildered, and Miss Bruce hesitated before acting. She sent a pupil go to pick up the principal. At last he entered, and the physician showed in a few minutes later. The physician determined they required hospitalization right away. Ambulances arrived shortly after and took them away. An ambulance arrived, and someone brought the boy to the principal's office.

When his mother arrived, she said nothing to him. It was not the right time to be upset, and she wasn't angry. So she just waited, watching.

Mr. Hensley demanded to know "why did you do this to those children" as he began questioning Whitey.

"I did nothing to those boys," he retorted.

One of the youngsters was the son of the school's principal, Mr. Hensley. "Miss Bruce, tell me what you saw."

"Whitey, why do you lie so much? Don't deny that I witnessed you hit those boys with that sock you had.

Sticking to his account, Whitey said, "I did not do it." One boy was invited to attend the meeting by Mr. Hensley. When Whitey attacked my son, Jerry, were you by his side?

"Yes, master."

THE ENGAGEMENT RULES

I think there are a few rules that need to be followed before we get started. If one wants to start with the appropriate mindset, these are some of the most crucial characteristics that both men and women should adopt.

1. Ask for what you need, want, and require with assertiveness. Like any other skill, assertiveness requires practice to become more proficient. Aggression and assertiveness are two different things. It involves taking the initiative, speaking honestly, and communicating.

This type of communication skills was not taught to many of us when we were growing up. It's possible that people like our parents discouraged us from voicing our opinions. That, in my opinion, contributes in part to why dating can be so difficult. How can we expect someone to live up to our expectations if we are uncomfortable asking for what we need and wanting?

For instance, those who bemoan their placement in the infamous "friend zone" do so because they lack the courage to be forceful. Declaring your plans up front can be scary, but what have we got to lose? Would you rather keep your feelings to yourself and lose someone you truly adore to someone who has the guts to pursue them? Women are known to like self-assured males who aren't afraid to express their emotions and intentions. Of course, guys are drawn to this as well. Men should initiate relationships, despite social standards to the contrary; these are older-generation behaviors. Simply said, they don't always work in today's dating environment. In reality, women have a set period of time on a well-known online dating app to initiate contact when they connect. If not, your match will vanish off the face of the earth.

Either of them can take the next step once she extends a friendly greeting.

Please have the maturity to tell someone if you are not feeling something for them, even if they have feelings for you. Tie up someone else's heart and head and keep them hanging while you search for someone else is unfair to them. Some people will stick with someone and play with their emotions until they meet someone they think is "better." If you are aware of this from the start, you can steer clear of pursuing someone who is just mildly interested in you. You are probably in a one-sided situation if the relationship is not developing or if you feel that you are putting in the most effort. Someone shows a lack of interest if they are not trying. Clearly. You have a plethora of reasons to justify yourself, but if someone is not prioritizing you, the solution is standing in front of you.

Be forthright and truthful.

Genuineness is essential. How can you possibly make someone fall in love with the real you if you are not being true to who you are? You will never be content if you try to give in to what you believe they desire. Your real self will eventually surface, and they'll tell their friends, "She was incredible before we got married." She instantly changed, and I lost all identity in her. Being honest about who you are and what you're searching for is something you owe to both yourself and everyone you encounter. As you progress, it can only be beneficial to the relationship. If something about someone isn't working out, talk to them first and try to work things out. Do they listen to what you have to say? You can very well assume that if they aren't at first, they never will be.

3. Have a gray perspective on individuals.

Have you ever thrown caution to the wind and thrown caution to the wind, only to find out later on that the person you fell in love with was not who you thought they would be? When you initially fall in love with someone, it's normal to unconsciously ignore their shortcomings. We elevate them to a pedestal and idealize their qualities due to our attraction to them. We overlook the fact that character is never clear-cut. Everybody is flawed, yet emotion can blind us to these imperfections. Admit the warning signs you observe in other people. If you want to avoid the possibility of being alone, it is far too simple to try to push yourself into a relationship that is not quite suitable for you. Avoid putting yourself in a situation where a relationship isn't fulfilling. Attraction and anxiety can have a lot in common. Recognize the signs and feelings of genuine attraction to ensure that you are not misinterpreting it due to loneliness or fear of losing someone. There's no way you'll meet someone else if you stay longer than you should.

4. Refrain from controlling others.

It might not be obvious when you are trying to control someone unless you examine your own behavior closely. When the word "manipulation" is spoken, thoughts of lying, cheating, or purposeful attempts to control people come to mind. However, in social situations, it is typically more nuanced. You are probably attempting to influence someone if you are attempting to get them to feel a different way about you. Manipulation may postpone or mitigate the final rejection if someone isn't into you, but it will never make them fall in love with you. People tend to behave emotionally and then analyze their actions, especially when it comes to dating and attraction. You can't make someone like you with logic. Chasing and controlling someone else can cause you pain and be hard to resist, but in the end, it will always be detrimental to your self-esteem. Additionally, you will make a relationship last far longer than it needs to.

5. Don't waste time on those who can't handle their emotions.

If someone is not showing you enough respect or interest, or if you are being treated poorly, leave. Never let someone step over a line with you that you wouldn't stand for in the case of a loved one. We can tolerate poor treatment of ourselves so well, but if we witnessed a buddy engaging in such conduct, we would never put up with it.

Recognize that you might not be connected to someone's lack of interest. You can never be too sure about someone's past dating experiences, underlying desires, or emotional tendencies.

6. Develop a beautiful farewell.

Don't waste your time on someone who doesn't return the favor. It's a waste of time and energy. When there is true attraction between you two, emotionally accessible people will accept your advances. The best method to keep your dignity intact when dating is to demonstrate that you are self-assured enough to leave a situation in which you are not being treated fairly. You can lie to yourself on a conscious level, but you can't trick your subconscious. It's critical to act as though everyone is observing you because, in actuality, they are. Keep in mind that everything you send or receive via email is permanent. Don't leave an enduring record of your disintegration. You'll be sorry you did.

7. The moment it ends, it ends.

You can tell when you're not getting the respect you deserve when it comes from your gut. There are various reasons why people remain in bad relationships, but at the core of the problem is the fear that we won't find someone better and would be forced to live a lonely existence. Additionally, be sure it is truly ended when you finally accept it and decide to end it. Your self-respect will only be weakened by obsessing over someone who got away or punishing yourself for attempting to make sense of what happened. Never let another person's actions to alter who you truly are, and always be true to yourself. If you do choose to end a relationship, maintain your composure and your dignity.

Following these guidelines will enable you to make wiser choices when it comes to dating. You stand the best chance of drawing similar traits in a mate if you conduct yourself with authenticity and maturity. These rules will assist you in maintaining a healthy degree of self-respect throughout time, and anyone you do end up getting married to will appreciate your self-assurance.

Eva ponders for some time. Is this dud my frog, and can we kiss to find out? Already 15 guys, 15 kisses. One more is harmless. She considers her options.

Without waiting for a response, Ethan gets up, takes Eva's hand, and leaves the cafe. Eva is distracted by his touch and walks hand in hand in confusion.

Ethan holds her face and asks her again while peering into her eyes as they exit the eatery.

Could you please visit my home?

Eva watches, closes her eyes, and gives Ethan a kiss. With a slight inclination of his cheek, Ethan gives her a kiss on the neck.

"No, Ethan, I'm unable to come. I need to finish this project." Eva retracts her steps and speaks in his mouth. Thankfully, it's not him. Salads and protein smoothies are spared me.

"Are you certain?" Ethan asks, putting his lips to her corner and embracing her.

"Yes, I'm fairly certain," Eva says, taking another step back. I'm done wanting the salad.

"I need to hurry Ethan up. My parents are quite understanding when it comes to my being out late. You are aware of parents. Eva lies once more.

"Should I take you home?" Ethan queries.

Yes. That is going to be fantastic. And they stroll to his car, says Eva.

While Ethan proudly drives her in his BMW, Eva is both thrilled and cursing Ana. "I wouldn't have had to deal with the salad and protein and football brouhaha if I had kissed him earlier." Eva gnaws at her idea.

"You know Eva, your kissing rule is just incorrect. She can hear Ana's voice in her head. "Mr. Wrongs are numerous and must be dealt with before meeting Mr. Right."

"Stop being so corny."

"Are you referring to yourself? You are giving Princess a frog kiss!

Eva chuckles at the irony of her life.

"Would you mind telling me the joke?" Ethan touches her just above the knee and whispers, wryly. Eva is caught off guard by Ethan and springs into her seat.

Nothing. I just realized an old joke. Eva firmly pulls her lips together, stepping back from his hand and slouching her leather sling bag over her knee. He's terrifying me now! And I feel stuck inside his vehicle. I do not wish for this to be a rerun of the Edward episode. No, no, no. Unaware that she has begun humming No..No..No..like a tune and moving her head along with it, Eva begins mentally repeating the phrase.

"Whoa, Eva... How are you spending your time? He brings the vehicle to a stop. "How are you doing?"

Eva pauses, focusing on his lifted eyebrows and popped eyes.

"What took place? You stopped the car, but why? She queries.

"I assumed you were having an asthma attack or something." He states. "You are so strange. a member of your kind. His lips are twisted. Not overjoyed to see her healthy, robust, and attractive.

"You desire for me to be ill?" Eva tells him to take his eyes off of her.

Not at all. Why not? Ethan scowls.

"So you can be my man and take care of me?" Eva speaks, crossing her fingers. Please become agitated and accelerate. She imagines.

Ethan rolls his eyes. What an oddball person she is? He speeds the car while considering. He drives directly to Eva's house without turning to look at her again.

"Ethan, thank you." As she gets out of the automobile, Eva extends her hand in farewell. He quickly waves and heads off.

With a sigh, Eva makes her way up the stairs to her room. Subsequently, she collapses onto the bed while her heels thump in a corner. Eva lies on the cushion and dials a call on her cell phone.

"Ana, I'm coming over here tomorrow." Eva says over the phone.

"I was anticipating your call." What was his state of mind?

"All I know is that I have no desire for the Greek God." Eva is self-pitying. "Hey, I followed your suggestion. Later on, I kissed him. She then chokes. "He's not the right one," Eva bursts into tears over the phone. "Ana, I will see you tomorrow." I'm going to hang up. Goodbye. She hangs up the phone, tears streaming down her face, not even listening to Ana. I'm over this garbage.

She lets forth a mental scream. Not any longer. Not any longer... With the sour recollections of numerous kisses but not a single loving moment, she mumbles as she goes to sleep.

Chapter 4: Difficulties and Obstacles

The challenges and issues that any romantic connection faces are covered in Chapter 4. It's a pivotal moment in the story when the characters realize that love is often characterized by trials and hardships rather than being an easy path.

The context for the struggles the protagonists will face is established at the beginning of the chapter. It could involve outside problems like miscommunications, conflicts, or pressures from friends or relatives. These challenges put their friendship to the test and force them to confront issues head-on.

We witness the heroes' emotional difficulties and development as they overcome these challenges. People may start to doubt their feelings, mistrust the connection, or even wonder if it's worth the effort at this point. This chapter provides a deep and poignant look into their minds and feelings.

The protagonists' tenacity and will are highlighted. Do they come up with strategies to get past difficulties, grow from their mistakes, and come out stronger as a team? Or do these difficulties serve as a tipping point that makes them rethink their partnership?

We look at the concepts of compromise, forgiving, and personal growth in Chapter 4. It's possible that the characters will need to learn to forgive and accept one another's flaws. They might also need to grow as individuals inside the partnership and adapt to new situations.

This chapter ought to additionally address the outside factors that contribute to their problems. These could be obligations to others, stress at job, or issues with family. By doing this, readers may relate the book to their own relationships and experiences, making it more approachable.

Difficulties and obstacles are a typical element of the path of love. They put the characters' commitment, ability to communicate, and flexibility to change to the test. In the end, Chapter 4 addresses the idea that strong love is defined by the characters' resolve to overcome obstacles in order to make their love tale even more enduring and significant.

I wanted to go loose and a little untidy with my hair while wearing a peach bandana dress. I accessorized my ensemble with these amazing heels. I thought that, having agreed with my dad that going to Thackeray College would be a fantastic chance for me, I had half the confidence that I had lost back. After all, he was an alumni.

I was enraged not to receive an invitation. I had no regrets, even though I knew that it might have been related to the gap year I took. I decided it would be better to come up with a plan to establish my own identity and rebuild my reputation than to wallow in self-pity. I was so excited when Arianne invited me to this party that I glowed.

I had to introduce myself because Arianne had already left my side to talk to some folks she knew from high school. I moved about the room as though I was the owner. As I strutted my stuff, the boys gazed at me, and the girls flocked to inquire about my costume. I was aware that the key was to present oneself well.

You were a cheerleader, then? And a president of the student body?" inquired Allison, a pink-haired girl.

I chuckled. "Yeah, that's right. That was in high school, though. Following college, I took a year off and traveled throughout Europe.

"Whoa! Mickey commented, "I'm so jealous," as she ran her hand over my dress' fabric. She questioned, "I bet you bought this there."

I informed her about the store I went to and nodded.

Mickey abruptly stopped speaking and made a lip-move in the direction of someone. When I looked up, I noticed a stunning brunette female with long legs approaching us. She had slanted eyes that gave her an almost nasty expression, and she was tall and fair. She was wearing a small tight dress that was the color of blood, so it was clear that she enjoyed showing off her curves.

"Therese Ford is that. Mickey muttered, "She's rich and has serious attitude problems," and we both laughed.

Therese approached us with assurance. She grinned as she gave me a look.

Hello. I had to come say hello to the girl with the amazing dress! Therese is my name. You are?" she questioned, taking hold of both of my hands.

I grinned. "Hey Therese! You've been talked about a lot. My name is Natalie.

Yes. I'm hoping for the best. She pouted and grinned once more. "I'm getting people together for our game of kiss or dare. Would you like to go with us? She gave a wink.

My newfound buddies encouraged me to go when I looked at them. Who would, of course, turn down an invitation from Therese Ford?

Indeed! I responded.

Fantastic!

Other students had gathered around the center as she dragged me in. A large rectangular couch with room for about twenty people was present. Allison, who was also invited by Therese's friend, sat next to me. The couch quickly filled with a variety of people, including gay men and lesbians in addition to boys and girls. To play the game, Therese took out a pricey bottle of rum.

The game was extremely easy. They would ask you to perform something while spinning the bottle. You would have to kiss someone if you said no. The challenges were really trite. To put an end to the celebration, some of them had to shout, dump drinks on someone, sing, or dance. I was glad that the dare I received was to smack a rugby player in the arm and tell him I saw a bug since I was giggling the entire time. I was enjoying myself greatly.

Then, as people started refusing challenges and kissing each other, the game become more competitive.

Therese told Allison, "Kiss your love interest of the night when you hear the word pool."

After chuckling and saying, "Easy," Allison drew the man close to her and gave him a deep kiss. My eyes widened, and I became hot to the touch as I saw her slide onto his lap. The audience applauded as they kissed for a long time.

He's such a wonderful kisser, damn it! Allison licked her lips and whispered as she withdrew.

The game went on. The most attractive man in the room was the target of Therese's second bottle spin. His hair was dark golden and brushed to the side; it was a touch long on top. I was staring into his bluish-green eyes, lost in a daze. For some reason, he reminded me of someone, but no matter how hard

I tried to remember where I had seen him before, I was unable to place him.

After observing him for the last half hour, it appeared that he was not genuinely engaged in the game. He was largely silent, but he laughed every now and then. I also saw that he exuded a powerful presence. The girls couldn't take their eyes off of him even though he didn't say much.

The texture of his white shirt gave the impression that his muscles were strained. Despite his minimalist appearance, he exuded sex appeal with his black jacket and pants. He was sitting there grinning, and he looked magnificent.

Therese appeared ecstatic. The girl who was going to dare her got a slap on the hand. "I'll pull it off!" she cried. She batted her eyelashes and tucked her hair behind her ears. She was obviously drawn to him.

With confidence, she declared, "I dare you to take off your shirt or kiss the most beautiful girl you've seen tonight."

It just lasted a moment, but he appeared shocked. Therese performed well since the girls would gain from his decision, whatever he made. My body tensed up as our gaze locked. When I thought of his kissing me, my heart began to pound so hard.

He got up and started to move toward me. He brought his face down to mine, and Allison shrieked with excitement. I was at a loss for what to think. His palm across my cheek was so callused that I lost all sense of smell. His powerful jaw was tight. With closed eyes, he carefully took hold of my lips.

When his lips moved in such a seductive way, I let go of everything. He gave me a slow, gentle kiss, and I couldn't help but desire more. I parted my lips to press the kiss a little more, wanting to taste his flavor. I pulled him in by putting my arms around his neck. I felt his knees next to my thighs and realized I was leaning against the couch's backrest with him on top of me.

He tasted sweet and minty, and his kiss was addictive. I moaning in his mouth, he suckled and bit my lower lip as his tongue twisted and spun inside my lips, without missing a single corner. I returned the taste to his mouth by inserting my tongue there.

I was so engrossed in the long, intense kiss that I didn't realize the game was still in progress. When we broke off the kiss, we were panting heavily. His forehead touched mine as he gave me a fiercely passionate and endearing look. I jolted back to reality as I heard a loud cheer.

I gave him a little shove. All of a sudden, nobody was acting rationally. He was punched and taunted by the hockey team. I occurred to glance at Therese, who was glaring at me and talking to her buddy.

Reed

"Look, I have to go give a quick speech over at the elementary school. Would you mind following us? I tug on my shirt's sleeves after straightening my cufflinks. They had become somewhat disheveled after I had assaulted her in the schoolhouse. Completely worthwhile.

Her mouth tightens. "At this point, you could ask me almost anything, and I would say yes."

For once, blissed out and at ease, I love her the way I do. Although I also enjoy her rough side, Karisma is exclusive to me in this regard. I don't believe for a second that Jeffrey, the self-centered jerk, had ever tried to hurt her feelings. It's likely that he was preoccupied with devising strategies to turn her intelligence, determination, and striking attractiveness into a valuable asset from which he could profit. She had always been viewed by him as a checklist rather than as a real person. After that, they split up, and I was left to pick up the pieces.

"Take caution, my love. If you're feeling so strongly yes, you have no idea what I might ask for.

Her eyes slowly open, glazed over with the enjoyment I have brought to her. Reed, I'm feeling very much yes. So kindly accompany me to your lavish, sensual mayor address.

I laugh, and together we make our way to the elementary school. Our school recently received additional federal funds, and I'm committed to seeing that it's put to use so that every student has access to technology in the classroom. I can't wait to announce to my town what Valentine's next plans are.

Upon our arrival, I notice multiple news vans and a few reporters pre-arranged with field and video reporters. It was unexpected, particularly considering that the pair was from Indianapolis, but I suppose Maryanne set it up because my reelection campaign was now formally under way. She is far more invested in this whole thing than I am. As Valentine's mayor, I believe I did a decent job, so I don't really need to worry. Maybe when the contest for governor comes up, I'll start to get concerned.

Senator Brian von Esrington is positioned at the podium, with Principal Kettelbaum standing next it. Whoa. Although I don't agree with the man's politics—he is heavily biased toward big business and old money—I am quite impressed with Maryanne's level of diligence in this matter. Undoubtedly, she is receiving a raise.

I turn to face the gathered throng and, much to my surprise, the senator is already speaking. "Now is the moment for Valentine to advance and move into the future. Each and every student at Lakeland Elementary will have access to a laptop for use in the classroom thanks to the federal funding that I personally assisted in obtaining for Valentine. We'll be able to provide coding and programming lessons, giving our kids a better future.

"What the hell," I growl.

Kar glances at me, her forehead furrowing with concern. Reed, what's going on? Why does Scrooge McDouchebag claim to be the innovator of your technology financing program?

"I'm going to find out, but I'm not sure." I stand up straight after leaning over to whisper with her, squeeze her hand lightly, and then move through the throng in the direction of the podium.

"Senator von Esrington, thank you so much for coming to Valentine." I give him a savage handshake while grinning at him.

"All right, all right. Harrington Reed. You are really gracious to come to my news conference today. Few men would treat their opponents with such courtesy.

Thank heavens I was raised by parents who instilled in me the value of never displaying any emotion on my face. The parts fall into place so swiftly that I feel like I've been smacked on. No one, including myself, saw this coming, but it doesn't mean I can't manage it. In addition to being a terrific mayor, I love Valentine. No matter how wealthy and sleazy he may be, no one can take that away from me.

Nonsense. Given that my own address is scheduled to begin in a few minutes, it only seems logical. I smile at him like a politician. The fucking fool's nerve. "You're going to be done by then, right?"

He glares at me like a reptile. "We'll undoubtedly be done in a short while. If you will pardon me now. He dismissively waves me off. Though I want to hiss in response, I decide that it will seem better if I play the gentleman and he is the jackass. I approach the Principal on the other side of the stage.

The Principal steps back from me a little. "I apologize, Reed. I felt unable to refuse the senator, even though I had no idea what this was about.

I sigh. Josh Kettelbaum is someone I like, and this isn't really his fault. "Don't worry. I understand. After that, I return to the sidelines and wait for this jerk to stop.

Like his previous speeches when campaigning for the Senate, this one is laden with self-congratulation. For the first time, I wonder what's going on here as he goes on and on about the government financing effort that I personally navigated through a mountain of paperwork to make happen. Von Esrington is obviously running for Valentine mayor, but what does a powerful D.C. financier want with my hometown?

I hear my name called again by the senator, startling me out of my reverie. This time, he's nearly shrieking, spittle flying from his mouth, and he's not even looking at me. Hold on, what? When did kids' use of technology turn into a contentious political issue?

"What have I missed?" I speak softly to Kettelbaum. With a distinctly ill-colored face, he takes another step away as his eyes dart from the senator to me.

A slideshow of pictures of me with different attractive women on my arm at various fundraising and charitable events is displayed by the projector. I'm still baffled by the whole situation. Shouldn't we be discussing the new computers with our primary school students? How is that related to my attending charity events?

The picture then pans to a picture of me mooning the camera while I was an undergraduate, dressed in a toga. Everyone in the room gasps, and the children all break out into loud giggles. What? The. Fuck. "That's enough for now."

"I'll state that it is. Mayor, the people of Valentine are sick and tired of your playboy behavior. It's time to elect someone with some decency and morality to the office—

I walk confidently toward him on the stage, then reach over to unplug the projector. I declared, "That's enough."

"Harrington, are you worried that everyone in the town can see you for who you really are?" His frigid, reptile eyes glitter as they look at me.

"I am well-known in my town. Senator, show a little decency.

"Exactly my point. Show some civility at the mayor's office. Von Esrington, elect. And he exits the stage in a tangle of bodyguards and greasy charisma with a huge flourish.

I turn to face the throng, and the majority of people are staring at me as though I've grown a second head. or showed them my nude posterior. Alright, sh*t.

"Now that the theatrical part of my speech has concluded, let me discuss the exciting developments taking place at Lakeland Elementary."

"Mayor, do you not have an answer to the pictures that Senator von Esrington recently made public?" This is coming from an unknown reporter that has a sharp appearance and is dressed in a fresh-blood red outfit.

My lips tighten into a line, then loosen to reveal a smile. "Ma'am, I'm not in the sensationalist industry. All I have to say at this point is that I'm sad the senator seems to think that my dating life is more intriguing than what we're doing here in Valentine. My private life is totally private. As I clear my throat, I fervently want a sip of water.

"But it appears, Mr. Harrington, that your love life isn't all that secret after all? How many different women will you date before the election, really? The other reporters giggle in response to her strong rejoinder. What a pack of wolves. Although I have a good feeling that von Esrington has paid her to rile me up, I won't fall for such a trap.

Throughout my time in government and during my campaign, I have always made an effort to maintain a polished professional image, never resorting to defaming my rivals. I figured that this was part of what people found endearing about me, that even in the political sphere, I was a guy of integrity.

However, I am also aware that a lot of people feed off of these kinds of contrived, shady underbelly tales. They enjoy watching someone go down in flames and get a rush from seeing someone else's unwashed laundry exposed. It may not be private, but it should be. I'm not going to give up easily, and I'm not going to get down on their level to keep going. I haven't done anything that should disgrace me or the people of Valentine, and I won't say sorry for showing up at charity functions beside a number of attractive women. I fail to see how my past relationships are related to the mayor's office. I adjust my necktie. "Now, regarding the new funding for technology."

However, after capturing their soundbites, the media boisterously packs up their stuff and marches outside to get into their cars. Almost as distracting as the slideshow had been is the cacophony of their departure. I know enough, at least, to end the speech here and express my gratitude to everyone who has helped Valentine's youth.

It probably did seem a little sketchy because the pictures were taken throughout the many years that have passed since my undergraduate years. To be honest, though, I'm not into relationships. Never have I. I occasionally go out with a stunning woman, but I won't feel bad about being alone and sometimes getting lucky.

Kettelbaum's hand feels clammy and cold from perspiration as I shake it. He murmurs, "What are you going to do about this, Reed?" to me.

I give him a sidelong glance. He is a married father of five younger children. "Are you truly completing this task at this very moment? You have more luck than I do. I got this instead of the right woman because I haven't discovered her yet.

He gives me a somber shake of the head. Reed, you're going to need to put in a lot of work to get this fixed. Although I am grateful for all that you have done for our school, you appear to be a trashy party boy in the senator's photos. For the remainder of the month, I will be taking calls from parents in this school district.

I let out a deep sigh. "While I wasn't the one who created the mess in the first place, I wish I could undo the entire thing."

"Are you certain?" Then he gives a thin-lined mouth and shakes his head. You are aware that it is irrelevant. It makes no difference if I was also unaware of what was going to happen. You and I will bear the brunt of criticism for your incapacity to keep your pants up. Many thanks.

We turn to face the photographer of the local paper, both of us flashing the most agonizing smiles of our lives. When Maryanne hears about this fresh catastrophe, she will burst into flames.

I look around for K.T., but she's nowhere to be seen. I had to locate her right away and resolve the entire issue. We're still in the early stages of this, so I can't allow her get the false impression of what's going on. I want her to stop using me as an excuse if I ever shut down on her.

She's pacing outside, pulling at her hair absently, so I smile and wave off the last of the reporters before making my way to my car. I kind of secretly think it's pretty hot when she does this when she's really worked up. Considering that it reminds me of yanking her hair. I apologize; I'm not sorry.

I scream out to her, "K.T." but it just makes her pace faster and move more erratically. "K.T., hello."

Her mouth forms what must be some very nasty swear words as her eyes dart up to meet me. This girl had a dirty mouth, so dirty that it might make a sailor blush. Considering that she was raised by two real hippies, I find it hard to understand how she managed to use such strong language. However, it makes me feel a little bit hotter for her in all those inappropriate ways, exactly like when her hair is tugged.

"Red, what were we thinking?" She stops cursing and pacing and looks directly at me. "We put your campaign at risk because we were so foolish."

I let out a coarse sigh. "Please, let's not do this here. Let's head home, grab some pizza and beer, and watch a scary movie together while we discuss it in the car.

Not at all. Put an end to it. We cannot act as though nothing occurred here. To support his onslaught, Baron von Evil is attempting to get your job and portraying you as some kind of manwhore.

I lightly hold her shoulders. "Everything will work out. It's going to need some extra caution when it comes to things between us. After nightfall, no spanky, hanky panky.

She gives a fierce shake of her head. That won't do, and I'm sure you're aware of that. Kade, give up trying to be cute to get out of this.

I release her so she can get back to her pacing. Haha. I understand. Being extremely secretive, the slightest suggestion that she might be the next is making her nuts. "Look, Kar, none of those photos showed you, and none of them were recent." At least in that regard, there's nothing to be concerned about.

She lets out a noise that sounds like a moose shot. Since dumb Jeffrey finally crap the bed with her for the last time and completely crushed her heart, I haven't seen her this worked up.

"You huge foolish boy, you don't get it. You believe there are no repercussions if you go around slamming somebody across a desk, get caught on camera, and go about your business. However, there are always repercussions. Did you not pay attention to the entire Bill Clinton controversy?

I laugh, sultry and low. "Back then, I was just a child. To be honest, I had no idea what the heck was going on. However, I can endorse a campaign approach involving an office blowie.

"You are a pig." When I talk to you about important, adult topics, you hide your face.

"Kar, it was you who went to office blowie land. Not me.

She gives me a strong whack on the chest with her small hand. It just makes me chuckle more.

Reed, just for a second, be serious. We both understand that I will not be able to transfer my bar to any of the locations we have in mind. It's time for me to move on and make a fresh start. Before everyone in Valentine realizes you're nailing the town bartender, let's call this off right away.

My hand goes to her face and lightly follows its curves. "I still think tavern wench is a better term." She withdraws from me, and it stings that she does so voluntarily from my touch.

"I'm serious. I can't keep taking these foolish chances with you; I have too much to do. Bring me home so I may begin packing and move on from you. Once more, her flawless arms are crossed in front of her. She's buried in her thoughts, afraid of everything, and I can't help her. I want to take her in and ease all of her pains.

Still, I give it my best. "You do not impede my path. You never obstruct my path.

She sighs. "And I refuse to be one either. Rich Boy, let's get out of here. Right now.

www.ingramcontent.com/pod-product-compliance
Lightning Source LLC
Chambersburg PA
CBHW052150110526
44591CB00012B/1930